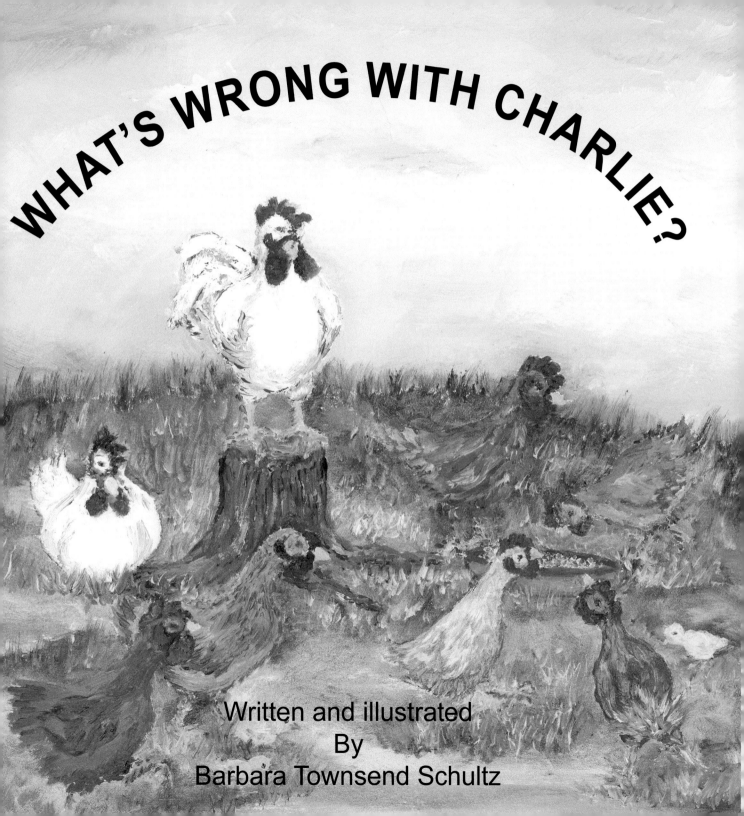

WHAT'S WRONG WITH CHARLIE?

Written and illustrated
By
Barbara Townsend Schultz

For John to fulfill a promise and for all my family and friends who believed I could do it.

Special thanks to Kathy Marshall for technical help and to people in the Thursday morning painting group for their encouragement every page of the way.

WHAT'S WRONG WITH CHARLIE?

Nothing much ever happened to Charlie.

  Day after day

  Same thing, same thing.

  Wake up the hens in the morning;

  Look out for them during the day.

  Next day.

  Same thing.

Nothing much ever happened to Charlie until the morning after a cold and chilling rain.

He awoke just as the sun was coming up, stood high on the fence post, and started to crow his morning "wake up" call.

er er uh uh guggle er

er, er, uh. uh, guggle!"

His throat felt raw and raspy. He tried again.

"er, uh, kkk, chuggle. ark, ark!"

Now he was really worried. His **"ER, ER, ER, ROO"** was nothing but a whisper.

Inside the farmhouse Sam rolled over in bed and asked his wife, Tillie, "Do you hear a strange noise coming from the chicken yard?"

"Come to think of it," she said, "I didn't hear Charlie this morning. Did you?"

They hurried into their clothes and out to the chicken yard. A droopy, worried Charlie was still trying to wake up the hens. But, all he could say was " er,er, erka, arka roooo."

Sam picked up his rooster and carried him inside. "Poor Charlie must have gotten chilled from all the rain and cold we've had."

"He must have a sore throat," Tillie agreed. "You fix him a box of clean straw by the stove. He can stay inside until he is better."

"Some cherry cough syrup might help," Sam added.

Tillie remembered that her grandmother used to make little balls of sugar and butter to soothe sore throats. She made some sugar balls and slipped one into Charlie's food pan every once in a while.

JUNE

S	M	T	W	T	F	S
				1	2	3	4
5	6	7	8	9	10	11
12	13	14	15	16	17	18
19	20	21	22	23	24	25
26	27	28	29	30		

HOME
COMFORT

Sam kept putting drops of cherry cough syrup into Charlie's beak. Charlie thought a little gingerbread would help more, so he helped himself when Sam and Tillie weren't looking.

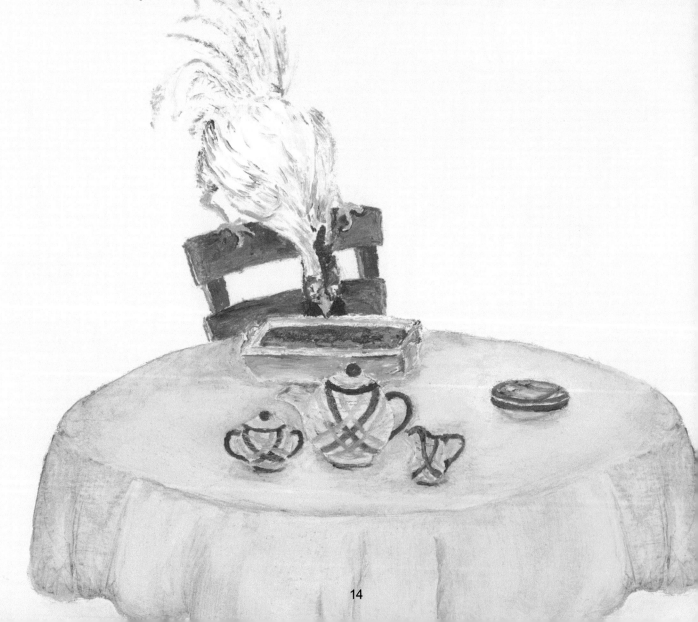

Every day he slept by the stove, drank cherry cough syrup,

ate sugar balls, had milk on his chicken feed, and picked

up wonderful things from the table—chocolate cake,

applesauce, buttered toast, blueberries . . . .

After several days in the kitchen, he awoke one day with a powerful urge to wake up the world.

"ER, ER, ER, ER, ROO!"

ER, ER

ER, ER, ROOO!

It was a wonderful, piercing sound that went through the ceiling.

It jarred Sam out of bed and onto the floor.

Tillie's eyes popped open.

They ran down the stairs and found Charlie standing on a chair and filling his chest with air for his "follow-up" crow.

"He's well," beamed Sam.

"Thank goodness!" Tillie laughed.

Sam carried Charlie back to the chicken yard. The hens crowded around him—so glad he was back home again. "Where have you been?" "What have you been doing?" "We missed you."

Charlie told exciting stories about the kitchen, the special kinds of food he had eaten, the cherry cough syrup, and the sugar balls.

"Sugar balls," they clucked. "We never heard of such a thing!"

"Cherry cough syrup. How wonderful!"

Days went by.

The hens grew tired of hearing about the kitchen. They began to doubt that there was such a thing as a sugar ball.

Charlie called his loudest every morning, but he got no special attention.

Day after day.

Same thing, same thing.

Wake up the hens in the morning;

Look out for them during the day.

Next day.

Same thing.

Ordinary food.

Dry, ordinary food.

Plain old water.

Nothing much happened to Charlie.

Every day was the same.

"This is a ho-hum life," he thought.

The next morning Charlie awoke just as the sun was coming up. He hopped up onto his fence post, let his tail feathers droop sadly down, and let his head and wings sag down.

Then in a low, scratchy, sickly voice, he called,

"er, er, uh, uh, guggle! er, uh, kkk, chuggle, ark, ark!

er er uh uh guggle er uh

To order additional copies of this book, contact:
Xlibris
844-714-8691
www.Xlibris.com
Orders@Xlibris.com

ISBN: Softcover   978-1-4535-1480-1
        Hardcover   978-1-4535-1481-8
        EBook   978-1-6641-3929-9

Print information available on the last page

Rev. date: 10/26/2020

Printed in the United States
By Bookmasters